COZY FRIENDS
CUTE & COMFY COLOURING BOOK
Coco Wyo

PENGUIN BOOKS

PENGUIN BOOKS

UK | USA | Canada | Ireland | Australia
India | New Zealand | South Africa

Penguin Books is part of the Penguin Random House group of companies
whose addresses can be found at global.penguinrandomhouse.com.

www.penguin.co.uk   www.puffin.co.uk   www.ladybird.co.uk

Published by Penguin Books in 2026

001

Illustrations copyright © CocoWyo, 2026

The moral right of the illustrator has been asserted

Penguin Random House values and supports copyright. Copyright fuels creativity, encourages diverse voices, promotes freedom of expression and supports a vibrant culture. Thank you for purchasing an authorized edition of this book and for respecting intellectual property laws by not reproducing, scanning or distributing any part of it by any means without permission. You are supporting authors and enabling Penguin Random House to continue to publish books for everyone. No part of this book may be used or reproduced in any manner for the purpose of training artificial intelligence technologies or systems. In accordance with Article 4(3) of the DSM Directive 2019/790, Penguin Random House expressly reserves this work from the text and data mining exception.

Printed in China

The authorized representative in the EEA is Penguin Random House Ireland,
Morrison Chambers, 32 Nassau Street, Dublin D02 YH68

A CIP catalogue record for this book is available from the British Library

ISBN: 978-0-241-80895-5

All correspondence to:
Penguin Books
Penguin Random House Children's
One Embassy Gardens, 8 Viaduct Gardens, London SW11 7BW

Penguin Random House is committed to a sustainable future for our business, our readers and our planet. This book is made from Forest Stewardship Council® certified paper.

COZY FRIENDS

Coco Wyo

This book belongs to

_____

COZY COLOURING COMMUNITY

Come say hi and be part of our supportive colouring community! Let's have fun together!

@cocowyocoloring

cocowyo.com

SHARE YOUR ARTWORKS

Let your uniqueness shine! Share your one-of-a-kind artworks with us. Don't forget to tag **#cocowyo** and **#cocowyocoloring**, we can't wait to see yours!

CUTE PATTERNS

Flower · Star · Plaid · Strawberry · Glitter

Use a blank sheet of paper when using marker or watercolour